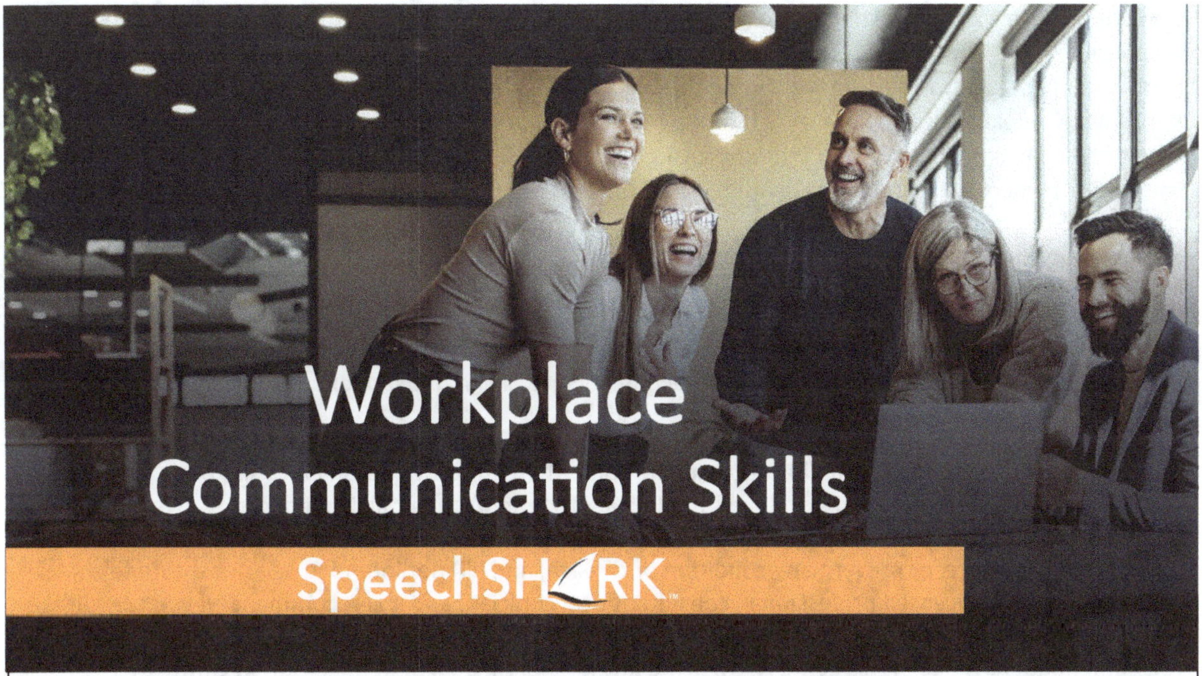

Workplace Communication Skills

Participant Handbook

Cover images © Shutterstock.com

www.innovativeinkpublishing.com
Send all inquiries to:
4050 Westmark Drive
Dubuque, IA 52004-1840

A Note from the Author

Participant Handbooks are designed to fully include all seminar content along with a copy of PowerPoint slides and class notes. Pertinent information is included, so students have access to materials that might not be included during shorter sessions. This allows for self-study and reflection following the seminar. To make the best use of this material, plan to participate in each section marked as a **Course Activity**. Read each question, consider the points, and answer them honestly. Fill in the blanks positioned throughout the book and internalize how these activities help improve your skills.

Facilitators do not have a magic wand to wave over participants and automatically transfer skills shared in a professional development session. Instead, it takes commitment and determination for the participant to learn skills and practice them repeatedly until the new skill becomes a new habit.

Best regards as you complete this workshop to better understand the nuances surrounding **Workplace Communication Skills** and their impact on your personal and professional development.

Course Objectives

During this workshop, participants will learn strategies for

Workplace Communication Skills that will aid in building relationships, sharing content, and becoming more sought-after employees.

Group Introductions

Have you ever attended a meeting where the room is filled with people you might not know? Often the speaker will begin by asking attendees to introduce themselves. Most people will say, "Hello! My name is (NAME) and I work for (NAME OF COMPANY) where I am the (NAME OF JOB)." At this point, the next person repeats the very same type of introduction. By the time you have listened to thirty people introduce themselves in this same way, you cannot remember many of their names, where they work, or what they do. Sure, some of them may stand out, but most of the introductions are lost.

How can you meet the challenge of a self-introduction when someone asks, "Tell me about yourself?" Do you have a plan? Would you like to know how to conquer this challenge? Afterall, this could be your grand opportunity for a conversation starter with a new colleague and a chance to network with others. Plan a 30-second introduction using the five-step template shown on the next page.

Step #1: Begin the introduction in a different position from all the others. For example, if everyone is sitting, try standing beside your chair. If they are all standing to introduce themselves, step into the aisle. Movement helps people remember who you are.

Step #2: Provide a greeting and start by asking a question or providing a quote that will help others connect with the type of work you do.

Step #3: Share your name but make the message memorable. Perhaps give them a way to remember your name.

Step #4: Avoid only sharing your company name; instead, **explain the value you bring to the company**. This proves credibility for your craft and will be the reason others want to start a conversation with you after the session.

Step #5: End with an upbeat greeting to let them know you welcome the chance to connect after the session!

Here is an example of how I introduce myself at a conference:

Good morning! Thanks for asking who I am and what I do, but do you mind if I ask you a question? Have you ever been to a conference and listened to a speaker who was great at sharing their message and passion for the topic? You know the speaker that I'm talking about, right? Well, I'm the person they hire to craft, rehearse, and deliver presentations that leaves the audience wanting more! My name is Dr. Penny Joyner Waddell, but my friends and colleagues call me SpeechShark. It is nice to meet you!

I hope this quick example will help as you introduce yourself at the next meeting or conference that you attend.

Course Activity: Use this area to write a *new* plan for introducing yourself.

Effective communication is the foundation for personal and professional success because it...
1. Builds _______________________________
2. Fosters Teamwork
3. Achieves _____________________________

What do employers want? They want and need Communication Skills and Soft Skills. According to the Graduate Management Admission Council (GMAC) Corporate Recruiters Survey, *"Communication-related skills remain among the top skills employers need."*

Course Activity: Let's Talk About It! Consider the skills you already have. List skills that your employer noticed about you during your job interview.

1.

2.

3.

4.

5.

6.

Course Activity: Listed are the top 15 Skills that GMAC discovered while conducting the survey. Place a check mark beside the soft skills and circle the hard skills.

How many of the soft skills are communication skills? _________________

How many hard skills are listed? _________________

List any additional hard skills you use in your current job position:
1.   4.
2.   5.
3.   6.

_______1. Oral Communication

_______2. Listening Skills

_______3. Adaptability

_______4. Written Communication – emails, letters, marketing, memos, etc.

_______5. Presentation Skills

_______6. Values Opinions of Others

_______7. Integrity

_______8. Follows the Leader

_______9. Drive – self-motivated, ambition, motivated, energy

_______10. Cross-cultural Sensitivity

_______11. Quantitative Analysis

_______12. Qualitative Analysis

_______13. Innovation and Creativity

_______14. Core Business Knowledge

_______15. Ability to Inspire or Influence Others

Employers want employees with hard skills to complete the job, but they need employees with __________ ________________ __________ and an understanding of **Soft Skills** to manage stress and uncertainty in the workplace.

The good news is that communication is a skill that can be learned.

Do you know what is involved with communication? It is more complicated than simply opening your mouth and saying what is on your mind.

Albert Mehrabian, author, instructor, and researcher, is best known for his theories regarding verbal and nonverbal communication. According to **Mehrabian's** research, fifty-five percent (**55%**) of our communication is determined by what we see. This could be anything from the color of your hair to the type of car you drive. _______________ percent of our communication is determined by what we hear. How we say a word or phrase carries more nonverbal cues than the actual meaning of the word. Volume, pitch, pace, rate of speech, inflections, pauses, vocal quality, breathing, and sighs are the vocal parts of nonverbal communication. And, yes, your accent is communication that we hear. Ironically, only _________ percent of our communication involves words. Ninety-three percent (**93%**) **is nonverbal,** and seven percent (**7%**) **is verbal**.

*This means that we believe what we **see** before we believe what we **hear**.*

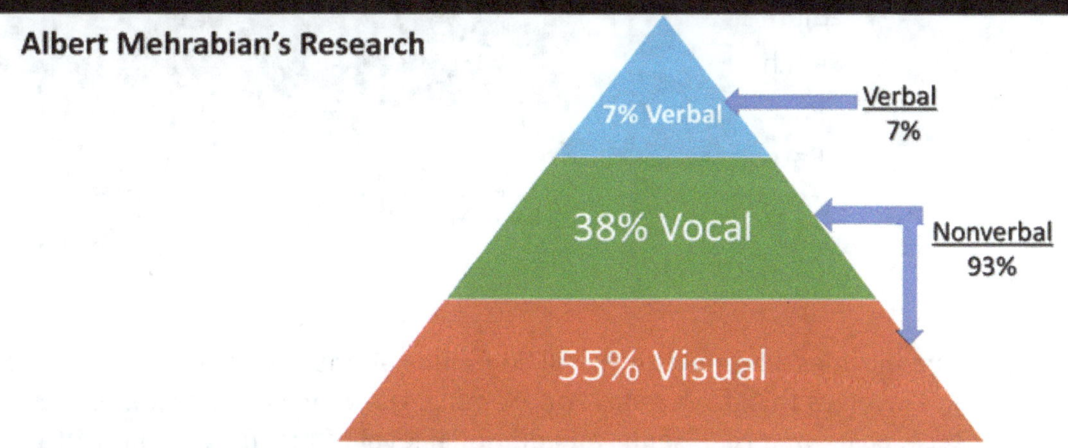

So, what is the definition of verbal and nonverbal communication?

Verbal Communication involves communication related to words whether spoken or written.

Nonverbal Communication communicates messages without the use of spoken language and is necessary for building relationships in personal and professional settings.

Cues are things we hear or see that serve as a signal, prompt, or hint of a situation or perception. Have you ever heard someone refer to **Nonverbal Cues** as **Body Language**? That's because we knowingly and unknowingly communicate messages without the use of words through cues and believe me when I say, "They speak volumes." Here are five forms of **Nonverbal Cues** along with a description of each:

1. ______________________
2. **Kinesics**
3. ______________________
4. **Chronemics**
5. ______________________

Paralanguage

Volume

Pitch

Pace

Rate

Color

Tone

Paralanguage includes all aspects of vocal communications that go beyond the meaning of words and involves things we hear. For example, the way we use *volume, pitch, pace, rate of speech, color, and tone* sends an additional level of meaning to the words during communication.

Have you ever heard of someone who was highly agitated, anxious, stressed, scared, or angry? Their paralanguage ____________ communicates emotions as well as a message. The same is true as you listen to someone who is calm or happy. While there are many subtleties of paralanguage, this element provides another layer of communication that can change or alter the meaning of the words used. This is why we often read into a message that is being sent to us. We check to see if the person's nonverbal cues in the form of paralanguage matches the _________________ used.

Course Activity: Let's Talk About It! Try reading these phrases and change your volume, pitch, pace, rate of speech, color, and tone.

You are so silly!

Are you serious?

Give me a Break!

Does the meaning change or remain the same?

Kinesics

Kinesics, another form of **Nonverbal Communication**, involves things we *see*. Think of how someone's *appearance* might change your perception of how they are personally. Whether we like to admit it or not, appearance can influence our ability to succeed. For example, a suitable appearance reflects positively on yourself and helps create positive first impressions. People who take care to groom properly, keep clothing clean and pressed, and wear clothes that fit, are perceived as trustworthy, competent, and sociable.

This goes much deeper than your physical appearance, but also includes posture, head tilting, and poise. How you present yourself *impacts* how others see you. This includes body movements and gestures. This type of body language communicates emotions, thoughts, attitudes, and beliefs. *Facial expressions* include ______ __________, *smiles or frowns,* and *head tilting* to communicate thoughts and feelings about the subject.

__________ ____________ studied the direct correlation of facial expressions involving smiles or frowns with emotions. His study confirmed that basic emotions produce their own unique set of natural facial expressions. To illustrate this point, Darwin studied blind children and realized that they smile when they are happy or frown and furrow their brows when they are sad or concerned. It is interesting to note that blind children do this even though they have never seen anyone use facial expressions to demonstrate emotions. In other words, a true smile communicates happiness in any language.

Much about **Kinesics,** such as appearance, posture, poise, and gestures, is a learned skill. However, other movements are *not* learned but naturally produced and recognized regardless of language differences, cultures, or by those who physically cannot see. Our true feelings are revealed by the way we _____________ and _____________ without using verbal communication at all.

What can we learn from eye contact? You can often, *but not always*, know what someone is thinking if you can read nonverbal cues sent through eye contact. First, consider the person's baseline behavior or the way they normally behave when not under stress. This should let you know if you can compare their behavior at this moment to the way they normally behave. It will also help you determine if something is not normal with their behaviors.

Various cultures or people with disability issues may have different actions related to their eye contact. Additionally, stress or anxiety can also produce the illusion that they are making up an answer, so be careful about jumping to conclusions or accusing someone of lying without a good reason.

Here are some basic things to remember when reading eye contact to know what someone is thinking: While visiting with someone, if they have strong eye contact and exhibit straight eye movement, then they are focused on what you are saying to them and are interested in your conversation.

How to Read Eye-Contact
and Know What Someone is Thinking

Straight Eye Movement
Thinking, Focused

Eye Contact that is straight ahead happens when someone is focused or giving serious thought to what is being said.

- **Up (_________):** As you notice someone's eye movement go up, then you know they are remembering or trying to remember something they have seen to relay to you in a conversation.
- **Center (_________):** As eye movement moves to the center, the person is remembering or trying to remember something they have heard to relay to you in a conversation.
- **Lower (_________):** Eye movements that move lower involve the person remembering or trying to remember something that deals with some type of body movement, body positions, or action. This might involve walking, dancing, driving, or swimming.

Looking to YOUR Left (their right): eye movement happens when someone is trying to _construct_ or _imagine something as possibly happening_.

- **Up (visual):** The person is _imagining_ images they might have seen.
- **Center (auditory):** The person is _imagining_ how something sounds. They may even be asking themselves, "Does this sound right?"
- **Lower (kinesthetic):** The person is _imagining_ how they might feel or how something feels.

Looking to YOUR right (their left): eye movement happens when someone is _remembering_ images or something they have experienced.

- **Up (visual):** The person is _remembering_ how something looked: a color, texture, or shape.
- **Center (auditory):** The person is _remembering_ sounds: a bird singing, their mother's voice, or children at play.
- **Lower (kinesthetic):** The person has an internal dialogue to _remember_ something through self-talk, perceptions, values, or beliefs.

_________________ is the study of how we use and understand physical space as we interact with others. It is a fascinating study of nonverbal cues that deal with the amount of space we place between ourselves and others. It also involves how much space we want others to occupy when they are moving into our space.

Space	Feet/Inches
Public Space	10-25 feet
Social Space	4-10 feet
Personal Space	1.5-4 feet
Intimate Space	0-18 inches

What does your use of space communicate to others?

Chronemics is an indicator of how we view time and how we use time. Are you always on time or chronically early or late? What about your friends or family members? This fascinating nonverbal cue involves human behavior and communication skills as it relates to cultural norms and expectations regarding time and the messages we send by our use of time. Perceptions of our own or others' punctuality, willingness to wait, and interactions that accompany this can affect our daily lives and relationships.

Understanding how we manage time, respond to messages, maintain punctuality, and communicate reveals how we view ourselves and those with whom we interact. If you are constantly late for meetings, dinner dates, appointments, or intimate gatherings with friends or family, you can bet that you are sending a loud nonverbal cue that your time is more important than their time. Sending delayed replies to texts or emails shows disinterest, preoccupation, and a signal that you are too busy for them.

Powerful messages are sent to others by the way we handle time. Arriving on time or a few minutes early for meetings communicates respect and commitment. Taking time to listen carefully to an employee or friend as they share a story with you shows empathy, care, and concern. Answering text messages and emails in a timely manner shows that you consider them and their message important and valuable.

Arriving on time or early for work, work appointments, and meetings will send a clear message to your boss that you value your job and have commitment to the organization.

Haptics is another nonverbal cue that communicates ways people and animals interact through touch. These positive cues are seen as people shake hands, fist bump, hold hands, hug, and pat others on the shoulder or back. They also send negative cues if it includes pulling, pushing, striking, or fighting. As a nonverbal cue, we can read someone's stress level by the way they adjust clothing, fidget with their hair, or wring their hands.

One of the most common forms of haptic touch in the business world is a handshake and it usually sends a message of goodwill. In the United States, it is a widely used form of greeting others and is considered as socially polite. Different forms of handshakes include:

1. **Extremely firm handshake** that displays ___________ ____________ and dominance.
2. **Firm handshake** that communicates confidence and support.
3. **Limp handshake** which communicates ______________________.
4. **Clasping both hands** over the other's hands communicates a high level of respect.

Following a meeting it is not uncommon for the members to share a brief handshake as they leave because it serves as the symbol of regards to one another. Following a game, the players on a losing team will line up to shake hands with the winning team as a show of good ______________.

Managers, teachers, and others who work with the public should be aware of how effective touch can be; however, care should be taken so that it is not misunderstood. A brief hand on the shoulder may be a nonverbal cue of support, care or empathy, but it could also lead to confusion regarding whether the touch was motivated by dominance or intimacy. The picture above demonstrates different types of touch.

Soft Skills

Verbal and Nonverbal

Intrapersonal Skills
Self-Awareness

Interpersonal Skills
Awareness of Others and Their Cues

Intercultural Skills
Awareness of Social and Cultural Differences

__________________**Skills** (self-awareness) are important soft skills that create an awareness of attitudes, appearance, character traits, confidence, self-motivation, time management, and work ethics. Maintaining integrity takes time and positive self-talk helps build character. Time management involves decisions based upon values you place on productivity. Additionally, creating a reputation of having strong work ethics relies on an ability to consistently perform in ways that produce results. Employers need people within their organizations that take time to be self-aware, so they understand themselves, their perceptions, attitudes, values, and beliefs.

__________________ **Skills** (people skills) include an awareness of others and their cues. People with great interpersonal skills thrive in work environments because they take time to consider how something they may say or do will affect others. Words that describe someone with people skills are proficient, competent, skilled, dependable, energetic, and devoted. These are also skills needed by employers as they create healthy environments.

__________________ **Skills** (social skills) refer to an awareness of various cultures and taking time to show interest and interact with people from other cultures. These people show empathy and compassion for others, seek to include others, and are flexible. Their intercultural abilities show strong problem-solving skills, adaptability, increased sense of curiosity, collaboration skills, and an interest in learning other languages. With our workforce becoming more diverse, adaptability is a needed skill and helps bring value to the organization as we work with a variety of customers, administrators, vendors, stakeholders, and peers. So, how are *your* communication skills?

How Are Your Communication Skills?

Listening and **Hearing** are surprisingly different. The graph below shows that listening Is an *actvity*, but hearing is a *process*. If you've never taken time to learn about this difference, refer to the comparison graph shown below.

Listening is an Important Communication Skill

Listening	Hearing
Activity	Process
Learned skill (taught and learned)	Response to stimuli and is involuntary
Requires the listener to be engaged, encode/decode, and respond	Passive and requires no action
Choice: requires focus and attention	If no hearing loss, hearing is continuous and ongoing
Message or content is consciously received and often gets a response	Sound is received but does not always elicit a response

Five Listening Steps to Know:
1. **Receive:** Focus on the meaning of the message as you receive verbal and nonverbal cues. Do the nonverbal cues match the verbal message?
2. ______________: Improve your message memory by intentionally processing the message delivered. Use a listening posture. Ask follow-up questions to test your understanding.
3. **Remember:** Refrain from judging the speaker or the message and focus on the meaning intended by the speaker. This helps you remember the message.
4. ______________: Focus on hearing the message by filtering out distractions and a mixture of incoming sounds. Be aware of perceptions and bias that can also cause distractions.
5. ______________: Verbal and nonverbal feedback is needed so that your response is effective and transactional. Effective responses that are kind, encouraging, and show concern allow the speaker to feel heard and valued.

Effective communication skills begin with effective ______________ skills so that you truly understand others, their emotions, perspectives, and the message they are sharing. There are five types of listening skills. Each one is important for various types of listening, but **Active Listening** remains the top listed skill needed by companies.

Using the **Listening Steps** in conjunction with the **Listening Types** helps improve the skill. For example, active listening refers to the transactional way we hear the message delivered and respond to the speaker's message taking into context nonverbal cues that are knowingly or unknowingly communicated. The following graphic shows a definition of each type of listening skill.

5 Types of Listening Skills

Active Listening:
listening to understand and observing nonverbal cues that match the speaker's message

Critical Listening:
resisting outside noise, distractions, personal feelings or perceptions of the speaker or the message

Empathetic Listening:
making an effort to see the speaker's point of view

Informative Listening:
making notes of main points, data, or issues

Appreciative Listening:
showing enjoyment of the speaker and content

Being an active listener is more than just being polite. It involves showing respect for the speaker and demonstrating with our body posture that we are showing a genuine interest in the speaker and the message. In other words, as we actively listen, we are creating an environment for trust, empathy, and concern that can lead to more productive conversations.

Improve your listening habits by using positive statements or asking open-ended questions such as the ones shown below.

- **Begin with a positive statement:**
  - I appreciate your perspective on this topic.
  - Thank you for sharing your thoughts.
  - I hear what you are saying.
  - That's a great point.
  - What I'm hearing is…"

- **Ask open-ended questions:**
  - Who is available on your team that can help?
  - What support do you need to move forward?
  - When can we meet to discuss this further?
  - Where do you think this issue is heading?
  - How does this align with your overall goals?

Providing ________________ or an appropriate ________________ is another way to show you understand the speaker's messages. **Paraphrase your understanding** of what the speaker said to show you understand their perspective and the message. Doing this reinforces understanding, encourages the speaker to continue speaking, clarifies any misunderstandings that may occur, builds trust with the speaker, and strengthens the relationship between the speaker and the listener. Following the conversation, ________________ the point of the conversation and show genuine care and concern for the information shared. Using **Active Listening Skills** in your personal or professional lives can help you become a more understanding, attentive, and empathetic listener. Why is listening important? Valuable workplace benefits are associated with effective listening skills. Not only will you notice (1) improvements in communication as relationships are strengthened, but this causes a ripple effect which (2) increases __________ as information is shared clearly and concisely, and (3) improves workplace morale, enhances empathy, and reduces conflict. Now, that sounds like a great skill to improve, right?

Questions	Never 1	Rarely 2	Sometimes 3	Often 4	Always 5
I pay attention to the speaker.					
I ignore distractions.					
I listen to a speaker's ideas without letting my opinions get in the way.					
I ignore distracting personal habits of the speaker (movements, sounds, actions).					
I take notes to organize the speaker's points.					
I think of questions to ask about unclear ideas.					
I understand unknown words from the balance of the speaker's message.					
I separate fact from opinion.					
I can tell the difference between important and unimportant details.					
I listen for the speaker to support points with research, personal stories, or examples.					
I respect that others may have different views.					
I evaluate the speaker and content of message.					
I get caught up in the story or emotions.					
I paraphrase what I've heard to clarify understanding.					
I try to feel what the speaker feels.					
I find hidden meanings revealed by subtle nonverbal cues.					
I use good listening skills and resist multi-tasking.					
If a speaker is struggling to explain something, I step in to assist.					
When people speak to me, I give head nods, smile, and offer verbal confirmations.					
Calculate each column: **Next, add the total of five columns together:**					

Now that we have covered listening skills, let's explore speaking skills for leaders.

"The art of communication is the language of leadership."
~ James Humes, Presidential Speechwriter

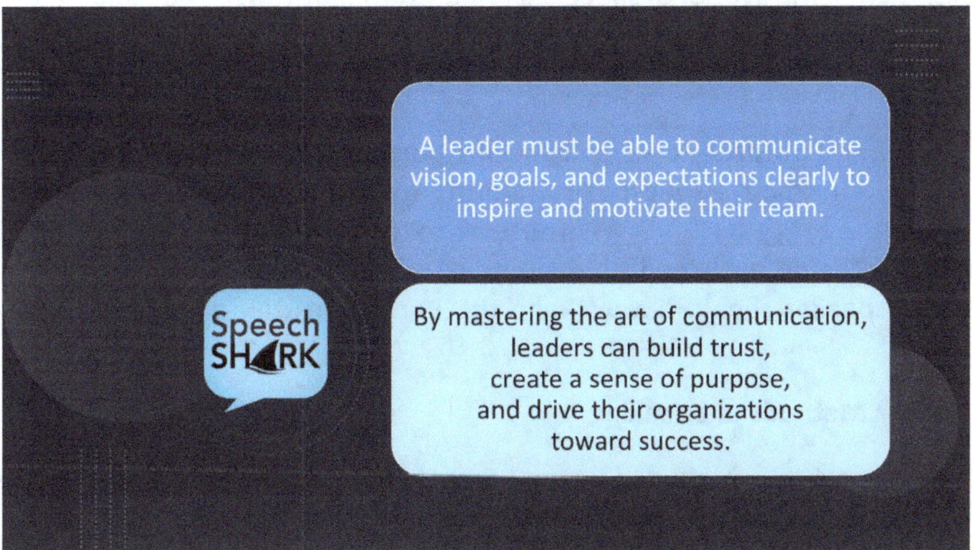

Leaders are constantly communicating through planned or casual conversations, presentations, or through written messages; therefore, the ability to communicate effectively is a skill every professional should develop. Since COVID, many of us have added online meetings to our regularly scheduled in-person meetings. They are convenient and time savers, but never underestimate the importance of face-to-face interactions for creating relationships that are crucial for good business.

Leaders communicate vision, goals, and expectations to motivate and inspire their team and to retain customers. By mastering the art of communication, we build trust, create a sense of purpose, and drive our organizations toward success.

Do you know how to plan a formal speech? There are general purposes, specific purposes, and methods for speaking along with various types of speeches.
Here are the three general purposes for presenting a speech:
1. ________________________
2. ________________________
3. ________________________

Informative speeches are given during meetings or informal gatherings to inform, explain, or demonstrate information. Leaders use this type of speech regularly during staff meetings or during interoffice conferences. **Entertaining** speeches are fun, lighthearted, and usually are reserved for special occasion meetings or in celebrations of accomplishments. **Motivational** speeches are used to motivate or persuade the team to prepare or complete specific projects, but they also are used to create energy for a task or project.

With each general purpose there is a specific purpose. For example, the ____________ **Purpose** of an informative speech is to inform, explain, or demonstrate a product or a process, but the ________________**Purpose** is to communicate the actual product or process that is being explained or demonstrated. As part of the speech preparation process, the speaker should always keep the **Purpose** as the guiding directive of the speech.

There are four **Methods of Speaking**:

Impromptu speaking can happen at any time when someone asks you to answer a question or if you are called upon to offer an explanation. This type of speaking comes with no opportunity for prior preparation, so it is a great idea to have a plan. The best plan is to always be *PREP*ared by using the P.R.E.P. model:
1. Restate your answer to the question as a main **P = POINT**.
2. Describe the **R = RELEVANCE** of the question to the situation described.
3. Share a current and relatable **E = EXAMPLE** to support your answer.
4. Summarize the **P = POINT** by restating it into the question.

Course Activity: Let's Talk About It! Use prepared questions for the class or Table Topics conversation starters. Allow each person to choose a question or card and immediately answer the question using the P.R.E.P. model. Celebrate each speaker and their answer by applauding as they enter and exit the stage area.

Example Question: If you could choose your favorite holiday of the year, what would it be and why?

Example Answer:
P = If I could choose my favorite holiday of the year, I would choose Thanksgiving.
R = I'm sure everyone in this audience has a favorite holiday, so this is a great question.
E = Thanksgiving is my favorite because it involves food, family, and friends.
P = So, that's why I would choose Thanksgiving as my favorite holiday of the year.

Extemporaneous speaking is work intensive, but many speakers prefer this because it allows time for the speaker to consider the needs of the audience, choose a topic that is relevant to the audience, research the topic, narrow the topic, create a presentation outline, create visual aids, and rehearse the speech before the presentation. One other important feature is that the speaker can have a presentation outline to take to the lectern as notes. With this type of speech, design opening comments that will grab the audience's attention, organize key points supported by personal examples or through research, and plan an ending that leaves the audience wanting more.

Manuscript speaking is a method that is often used by politicians or law enforcement officials when they need to share information that is precise and on-point. It is for this reason that the speaker will write the entire speech word-for-word and will ___________ the full speech using notes or a teleprompter. Even though the speech is read verbatim, it requires preparation by the speaker. Time must be taken to fully understand the content and purpose of the speech. ___________________ is imperative for the speaker to be comfortable enough with the content to use good eye contact, gestures, pauses when needed, and planned areas for emphasis. One major drawback for a manuscript speech is that the speech will sound like it is being read to the audience. It is advisable for the speaker to rehearse using a conversational tone so that the natural flow of speech is not broken. Showing expressions, enthusiasm, and a variation of volume, pitch, pace, rate, and color will maintain a ___________ needed to keep the audience engaged.

Memorized speaking is probably the least favorite of all speeches due to the trouble of memorizing a speech word-for-word. Basically, this is a manuscript speech that is memorized. This type of speech is particularly challenging when large amounts of __________ or __________________ need to be shared with the audience or if there is little prep time to memorize a full speech. Notes are not used during this method of speaking in comparison to extemporaneous and manuscript but can be used during occasions when you might want to offer the illusion of an organized conversation between yourself and your audience. Since it is memorized, it allows for more opportunities to gesture or to move about on the stage instead of being tied to a set of notes on the lectern. Comedians love to use this type of speaking because they can design the wording and add pauses or nonverbal cues to encourage laughter from the audience. Sharing personal stories and moments of inspiration would also be an ideal time to present a completely memorized speech.

Now that we have covered the methods of speaking, here are 7 types of speeches:

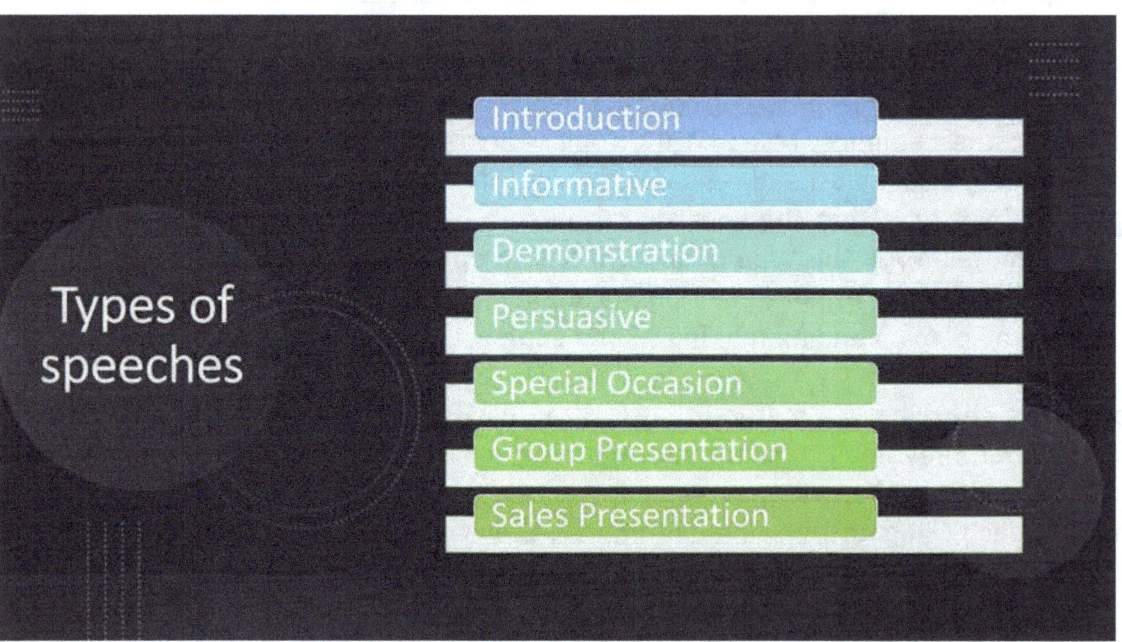

Different types require different planning strategies according to the purpose. For example, the **Introduction Speech** will usually cover three main points about the person or organization being introduced: (1) the past, (2) the present, and (3) the future. An **Informative Speech** will cover ____________ to __________________ main points according to the content needed by the audience.

A **Demonstration Speech** will cover three main points: (1) the history of the product or process being demonstrated, (2) materials required for the product or process, and (3) the demonstration. A **Persuasion Speech** and a ________________ ____________________ are similar and will cover three main points: (1) the problem with the status quo, (2) a realistic solution to the problem, and (3) the benefits of solving the problem or the consequences if the problem is not solved.

Special Occasion Speeches cover three areas: Social, Ceremonial, or Work-related speeches and are designed in keeping with the type of content the audience needs to hear. This leaves the **Group Presentation** which involves several participants along with a moderator that manages the presentation.

It's time to think about crafting and giving a speech! Regardless of the type or method of speech, every speaker should plan the presentation by completing the following:

1. **Conduct an audience analysis.** Consider their age, gender, level of education, interests, and anything else that will help you understand who will be hearing the speech.
2. **Determine the purpose** that meets the needs of the audience. Why are you presenting the speech?
3. **Select and narrow the topic.** Choose a topic that will interest your audience, provide ________________ information, or add to their existing knowledge.
4. **Conduct** ________________ **and gather materials.** Consider if you will need personal stories, data, or experiential research to support the topic. Do you need to speak to someone to get more information about the topic before it is presented? Do you need to create a PowerPoint or gather materials to use for visual aids?
5. **Develop the main points.** Understand how much time you are allowed to have for the speech and choose the main points that stay within the timeframe while offering information needed by participants.
6. **Create an introduction** that gets the interest of the audience within the first few seconds of the speech and then **Design a conclusion** that ends with a BANG!
7. **Rehearse and deliver the speech.** Plan to rehearse a minimum of three times. Change words that are not easily spoken, time the speech to make sure you stay within the timeframe and create presentation notes that are brief and easy to follow.

ALL Speeches Have a Common Design

I. **Introduction**
   A. Attention Step
   B. Establish Credibility
   C. Establish Relevance
   D. Preview Main Points

II. **Body**
   A. Cover Main Points
   B. Transitions

III. **Conclusion**
   A. Summary of Main Points
   B. End with a BANG!

Planning the **Introduction** includes designing a catchy attention step, establishing your credibility as a speaker, establishing relevance for the topic, and offering a preview of the main points you will cover. The **Body** of a speech details the main points separated by clearly crafted transition sentences. And the **Conclusion** offers a __________ of the main points covered, followed by ending comments that will challenge the audience, entertain them with a closing __________________, quote, or poem, or startle them with impressive data or a call to action. In any event, this part of the speech must be designed so that it leaves the audience wanting more.

Lots of people get anxious when speaking in public, but the trick is to plan, prepare, and persevere, but *never* tell the audience that you are nervous. If you don't tell them, they will not know, even though you think they will. This quote might help with that:

> **The human brain starts working the moment you are born**
> **and never stops until you stand to speak in public."**
> ~ *George Jessel (American actor, singer, writer)*

If you are ready to hear the applause, the trick is to rehearse, rehearse, rehearse! That means you should plan to rehearse a minimum of three times for each speech you give. This will give you time to change words that do not come easily, time your speech to stay within the expectations of the host and become familiar with the content.

For all the years that I've spent speaking and teaching students how to speak in public, I can say that this quote certainly rings true. No matter how much time you've spent writing a speech, rehearsing it, even memorizing the speech, it might still change a bit during the actual presentation. That's OK. In fact, you want your speech to sound like it's the first time you have ever given it. Speakers call this _______ ___________ ____ ____ __________ _____________. The more you practice, the easier it becomes, and you will soon begin to consider speaking in public as fun!

There are always three speeches for every one you gave: (1) the one you practiced, (2) the one you gave, and (3) the one you WISH you gave."
~ Dale Carnegie, Author and Instructor

Work-related speeches may involve any of the various methods of speech that we have already explored: Impromptu, Extemporaneous, Manuscript, or Memorized. They usually take the form of an **Elevator Pitch**, **Welcome Speech**, **Introduction Speech**, or it may involve an **Awards Ceremony**, but there are other types, too. All the various work-related speeches fall into the category of **Special Occasion Speeches**.

As you plan other types of speeches, just remember that most of them are short, light, and friendly. These provide opportunities for you to introduce yourself or others. Sometimes it involves opening meetings or conferences where you welcome attendees and introduce the agenda. In every case, it is a good idea to follow the 7 steps for planning a speech and create clear points that respond to your audience's needs.

Elevator Pitch

This short speech quickly introduces yourself to someone and is delivered in the time it takes to ride an elevator to the next floor.

- **Introduction:** begin with a greeting, handshake, name, job title, and personal tagline

- **Body:** explain why you chose this line of work, highlight experiences, strengths, show interest in listener, and present a business card

- **Closing:** ask for appropriate response for pitch, handshake, and thank listener for time

Course Activity: Let's Talk About It! Use this area and the template provided on the next page, to plan and present a 2-minute elevator pitch to introduce yourself. Be prepared to use the Elevator Pitch Peer Review to evaluate the performance of your classmates.

Elevator Speech Planning Guide:

Write a 2-minute elevator pitch. Even though you should plan this type of extemporaneous speech, it should sound unrehearsed. ALWAYS have one ready for job fairs, career expos, Facebook postings, LinkedIn or anyplace where someone might say, "Tell me about yourself." The following elements are required:

I.   **Introduction (one sentence)**
  - A.   Supply a greeting, your name, job title, and a personal tagline (examples below).
  - B.   Extend your hand for a handshake or other acceptable form of contact (head nod, fist bump, wave).

II.   **Body (two or three sentences)**
  - A.   Share briefly why you chose this line of work and how it fits with your goals and values.
  - B.   List top accomplishments and communicate achievements that make you proud and illustrate your contributions or problems you solved.
  - C.   Explain why people benefit from working with you.
  - D.   Share strengths and experience or how you bring value and contribute to the organization.
  - E.   Share the interest you have in the person to whom you are speaking.
  - F.   Present a business card.

III.   **Closing**
  - A.   Summarize what you hope to achieve from this brief meeting.
  - B.   Thank the listener and let them know you appreciate their time.
  - C.   Part with a handshake or other acceptable form of contact and an upbeat farewell greeting.

What is a personal tagline? This is not just a job title, but answers one or all the following questions: What do you do when you're working? What is important about the skills you have? What change do you make for others? What value do you have that is worth paying for?

Example of a tagline:

- I am an Accountant. I help people create a path for comfort and wealth.
- I am a Social Media expert. I build Facebook pages that help companies engage with customers.
- I am a Corporate Trainer. I help prepare local, state, national, and global industries for the workplace.

Elevator Speech Peer Review Sheet

Area	5 Excellent	4 Good	3 Average	2 Fair	Not Observed
Introduction Sentence: Greeting -------------------------------- Name -------------------------------- Handshake-------------------------- Job Title ---------------------------- Personal Tagline ---------------------					
Body Organized Pitch--------------------- Clear Details ------------------------ Information Focused/Effective--- Presented Business Card-----------					
Conclusion Restated Name---------------------- Requested Response to Pitch----- Share Appreciation for Time------ Handshake --------------------------- Farewell Comments----------------					
Delivery Volume----------------------------- Confidence/Enthusiasm----------- Appearance, Poise, Posture------- Language Skills---------------------- Gestures/Movement---------------- Would you contact this person to speak further?--------------------					
Total columns giving a score to each of the 20 line items:					

Welcome Speeches are presented at the beginning of an event and should welcome attendees and provide instructions. This is also a great time to introduce the ______________ or __________________ for the day. The person who conducts the welcome speech is also the same speaker that introduces the next event as it progresses on the agenda and keeps the meeting or conference running smoothly. While the announcements and welcome are short, they are also light-hearted, fun, and motivating.

Introduction Speeches

These are intended to introduce yourself or someone else. In both cases, the three main points should cover:

(1) The Past

(2) The Present

(3) The Future

Award Ceremonies are Special Occasion work-related speeches and are conducted in two ways: Accepting an award or presenting an award.

Accepting an Award is usually delivered as an ______________________________ speech since the award is not always announced prior to the ceremony. Without having prior notice, the honor should be accepted showing sincere appreciation for the award and the organization presenting the award taking care to pronounce names correctly. Including a personal story is a nice touch, especially if it also provides an opportunity to thank others who nominated you or paved the way for you to receive the award. In any event, keep the acceptance speech short and friendly.

Presenting an Award involves referring to the occasion, acknowledging the contributions of the recipient, and presenting the award with grace and dignity. It is a good idea to include a __________ ______________ of the award along with qualifications for earning the award. Deliver this short presentation solemnly and take care to correctly pronounce the name of the award, the organization presenting the award, and the recipient's name.

Let's Review:

- Overview of Sessions for 2025
- Workplace Communication Skills
  - Group Introductions
  - What Employers Want
  - Verbal and Nonverbal Cues
  - Intrapersonal, Interpersonal, Intercultural
  - Listening and Speaking Skills

Participant Handbook Answer Key

Page: 6
- Strong relationships
- Common goals

Page: 8
- Effective Communication Skills
- Thirty-eight (38%)
- Seven (7%)

Page: 9
- Paralanguage
- Proxemics
- Haptics

Page: 10
- Color
- Words

Page: 11
- Eye contact
- Charles Darwin

Page: 12
- Move
- React

Page: 13
- Visual
- Auditory
- Kinesthetic
- Proxemics

Page: 15
- Intimidation
- Dominance
- Weakness
- Sportsmanship

Page: 16
- Intrapersonal
- Interpersonal
- Intercultural

Page: 18
- Understand
- Evaluate
- Respond
- listening

Page: 19
- Feedback
- Response
- Summarize
- Productivity

Page: 21
- Informative
- Entertaining
- Motivational

Page: 23
- General
- Specific

Page: 23
- Read
- Rehearsal
- Rhythm

Page: 24
- Data
- Details
- Three
- Five

Page: 25
- Sales Presentation
- New
- Research

Page: 26
- Summary
- Story

Page: 2
- The
- Illusion
- Of
- The
- First
- Time

Page: 31
- Agenda
- Activities
- Impromptu
- Brief history

Icebreakers, Activities, Video Links and Supplemental Materials

- **Listen FIRST, Speak SECOND**: This is an Active Listening Skill exercise with the purpose of developing listeners who are listening to understand the speaker. Divide the group into pairs. Have one person share their experience with an unhappy customer while the other one listens: no interruptions, change in focus, no planning a future response. The second person should not interrupt, ask questions, or make comments until the first person quits speaking. Then, the second person can ask questions or offer suggestions to keep the conversation going. Ask the second person if it was hard to not respond or ask questions? Ask the first person if the questions were helpful. Ask if this exercise was difficult? Why or why not?

- **Will you listen to me?** This active listening exercise is designed as a personal listening development exercise. Send everyone out of the classroom area and to a busy part of the building. The objective is to seek out someone you do not know. Tell them you are part of a listening class and ask if they can help you with an assignment to have someone speak to you for twenty minutes to answer, "Who had the biggest impact on the person you have become and how has your life changed because of them?" Your job is to listen to this person speak for twenty minutes without asking questions, without offering responses, or providing head nods, smiles, or frowns. After the time is up, ask the person these questions: (1) How did it feel to have the freedom to speak for 20 minutes without interruption? (2) Would you prefer someone to respond or listen quietly?

- **Two Truths and One Lie**: Have fun reading body language to decide what is the truth and what is the lie. Use the full class or break the class into groups. Start by asking each person to come up with two true facts about themselves and one lie. Have one person stand and share their three statements. Everyone in the group will vote or discuss their guess for the lie. The speaker will reveal the truths and the lie.

- **How do we truly listen and make sure others are heard? With Simon Sinek**
  www.youtube.com/watch?v=60UOsgsmxu8&t=88s

- **How to actively listen to others? With Scott Pierce: TEDxBirmingham**
  www.youtube.com/watch?v=Yq5pJ0q3xuc

- **The 60 seconds that make or break a conversation with Chris Fenning: TEDxEindhoven**
  www.youtube.com/watch?v=rpFmRq5KeJs

- <u>How to be an Effective Listener and Why</u> – Dr. Manny Steil
  www.youtube.com/watch?v=8Ze98hf5Gjl

Thank you for allowing me to join your journey towards leadership. It is my sincere desire to share helpful and realistic strategies with you. I'm your author, Dr. Penny Joyner Waddell, but most of my friends and colleagues call me the SpeechShark. That's because I serve as an author, professional speaker, speech coach, and corporate trainer for local, state, national, and global industry leaders seeking to improve leadership and communication skills.

With a doctoral degree in Educational Leadership, an M.Ed in Instructional Technology Design with a concentration in Communication, and a B.A. degree in Speech Education along with experience gained through business, employment opportunities, and entrepreneurial endeavors, I have the background needed to facilitate professional development and continuing education seminars.

Designing, developing and presenting instructional content is a task which has provided lots of joy through the years. I'm the author of ***Basic Writing for Business*** and ***Going from Stress to Success*** (9th ed.) published by Pearson Publishers, ***SpeechShark: a Public Speaking Guide*** (4th ed.) and ***CommunicationShark: a Human Communication Guide*** (3rd ed.) published by Kendall Hunt, as well as the developer of the ***SpeechShark*** app designed to help people create, rehearse, and present speeches. Recently, I began working with Innovative Ink Publishers to produce facilitator and participant handbooks specifically designed for professional development seminar topics that enhance workforce readiness.

It was a supreme honor to receive the prestigious National Communication Association's Community College Educator of the Year Award, Georgia's Presidential Award from Toastmasters International, the Technical College System of Georgia's Rick Perkins Award for Excellence in Teaching from Gwinnett Technical College, and the coveted SkillsUSA National Educator of the Year Award for Career and Technical Colleges. While very much appreciated, these awards pale in comparison to the joy I feel when leading a seminar filled with industry leaders, managers, and staff members seeking enrichment to create a welcoming, professional, and enjoyable workplace.

For information or to book my services, please visit the website or contact me directly using the links below. I would also love to hear from you if you have suggestions of ways to make this a stronger course.

All my best,

Penny Joyner Waddell, EdD
www.SpeechShark.org
Penny@SpeechShark.org